COLORADO
JOHN FIELDER WILDFLOWERS

Photography and Words
by John Fielder

Colorado Littlebooks

Westcliffe Publishers, Inc. Englewood, Colorado

First frontispiece: Daisies proliferate along the
Stony Pass Road, Rio Grande National Forest

Second frontispiece: The first week in June brings
great fields of dandelions, Wet Mountain Valley

Third frontispiece: Paintbrush, Columbine, and
Larkspur cover the slopes of the Mosquito Range

Opposite: Paintbrush and Showy daisies drink from
Lake Creek, Sawatch Range

International Standard Book Number:
ISBN 1-56579-004-9
Copyright   1985, John Fielder.
            All rights reserved.
Published by Westcliffe Publishers, Inc.
            2650 South Zuni
            Englewood, Colorado 80110
Designed by Gerald Miller Simpson · Denver
Typographer Edward A. Nies
Printed in Korea by Sung In Printing Company, Ltd.,
            Seoul

PREFACE

Colorado is such a great place to be if one enjoys color. I don't mean yellow cabs and neon signs; I mean those colors that nature provides us through the plants that grow on our planet.

Each of those plants has a flower, and each of those flowers has a particular color, or colors, and the range of colors of all these flowers must be infinite in size. Here in Colorado we seem to be blessed with a great variety of wild flowering plants, especially in the wetter sub-alpine and alpine domains.

At least to the eye of a layman, this seems to be the case. To the eye of a landscape photographer, there is a wealth of colorful subject matter, and we strain ourselves to find it. And we usually do if it's there. One of the great joys for me in having been able to explore and photograph the Colorado landscape has been discovering wildflowers.

This book is not intended to be a "guide to Colorado wildflowers." There are numerous fine books that have been published locally that serve that purpose. Some have color plates, like this book, and are meant to be useful in identifying and naming wild flowering plants. I use one myself.

This small book is here merely for the sake of spreading a little joy through the medium of color photography. It is one man's visual interpretation of the Colorado landscape using a camera. It is an attempt to celebrate the spectacle of nature with emphasis upon wildflowers in our great state of Colorado.

I have chosen thirty-four of my favorite wildflower images, made over the past 12 years. The images chosen represent those scenes that I feel best display wildflowers within their alpine environment. Hence, there are not many close-up photographs, but mostly scenes depicting the landscape as you or I would see it with the normal magnification of the human eye. The images hopefully suggest feelings of "place," allowing the viewer to envision himself at the site.

All of the wildflowers that blossom in Colorado are not represented in this small book. To the contrary, I have come woefully short of that goal, and couldn't even accomplish that in a larger format book. However, many of our state's most popular species are represented. Indian paintbrush, Lupines, Columbines, Daisies, and Dandelions seem to be some of the more common, at least in the places I've visited. There are, of course, hundreds more, and only a walk in the woods is necessary to see some of them.

Wildflowers grow profusely all over Colorado, but especially in the alpine domains. Certain species bloom at certain times of the

Orange sneezeweed loses this year's life to early snows, San Juan Mountains

year only, while others seem to be around throughout the growing season. Certain species live only within narrow ranges of elevation, while others I've seen exist both down low and up high.

Some wildflowers grow in dry, sandy soils; others grow only in wet, boggy domains. Some wildflowers are incredibly small in size; others are as big as the garden varieties sold by the florist. In the past twelve years there have been "good" and "bad" years for viewing wildflowers. The good years seemed to have followed not only heavy winter snows, but also enjoyed consistent rainfall through the course of the summer. The bad years generally have followed dry winters and endured dry summers.

The past few years have been very good years for photographing flowers. In fact, I've had great fun making images of flowers in September, and even into October when the first snows have fallen around the flowers. There is nothing more beautiful that the reds of Indian paintbrush protruding through white snow, or snow resting on the petals of Colorado columbine, our state flower. Last year I photographed Orange sneezeweed wilting in the San Juan Mountains under the weight of six inches of wet October snow.

Probably the most fascinating flowers are those that grow only in the high tundras of the Colorado Rockies. The tundra is the dense, spongy matting of grass, mosses, and other plants that live above 12,500 feet (approximately). There, after the highest snows have melted, tiny wildflowers begin to bloom. Usually this does not occur until the middle of July, but the wait is well worthwhile. If you have never seen the iridescent blues of Forget-Me-Not, the whites and pale violets of Phlox, or the magenta of Alpine clover, a hike above the timberline is a wonderful experience.

Appreciating the things that nature has provided us in wilderness is one of the great ways to enrich our lives. For me, retreat to wilderness is a necessity. When I go there, whether to photograph or not, I enrich my experience by being vigilant. Colors, forms and shapes, unusual moments in time caused by light and weather, they all influence and stimulate the senses. Smells and sounds in wilderness do the same.

I hope this book, its photographs and words, stimulate the senses of those who view it, and fosters a great appreciation for the joy found in wilderness.

JOHN FIELDER

Showy daisies drink from an afternoon shower, White River National Forest

Beneath the gaze of distant peaks
Our yellows shine for so few weeks
It's such a shame our brilliance here
Can't be 'round throughout the year

False lupine below West Spanish Peak,
Culebra Range

Up close our petals seem to smile
Above the sea beyond a mile
Our scrawny stems they seem to be
About as tall as any tree

Nuttall sunflowers in the Wet
Mountain Valley

This flower's beauty is so great
It is the choice within our state
When friends they ask to know what's fine
I often say "the columbine"

Yellow columbine and Mountain Bluebell,
Sawatch Range

It's name so strange I can't guess why
Unless you have the nerve to try
To put your nose so very close
And breathe inside a heavy dose

Orange sneezeweed, Maroon Bells-
Snowmass Wilderness

With all the days of summer rain
We try to steal the forest floor
But when the wet begins to wane
Our roots they say they'll spread no more

Arnica, White River National Forest

Pale yellow do its flowers boast
In spring you tend to see the most
Its name implies it lives for snow
But underneath it will not grow

Snowlover and Bluebell, Mosquito Range

At home our lawns we try to spray
To keep these flowers far away
But when they grow across the hills
They are the last thing we would kill

Dandelions below Lizard Head Peak,
San Miguel Mountains

Across the valley they do spread
Without regard for where they tread
They'd best watch out for Farmer Fred
He'll hitch the plow and they'll be dead

Nuttall sunflowers below the Sangre de
Cristo Mountains

It is too late for I do fear
It's not the time to try to grow
For don't they see that it's quite clear
That Winter's here with all its snow

Indian paintbrush and Cinquefoil,
September in the Rio Grande National
Forest

They paint pastels across great fields
To nothing do they think to yield
And pink and green do complement
So when they spread we won't lament

Blue-eyed grass, South Park

This tree it left us long ago
Who'd take its place we did not know
So now we try to fill that space
With colors for a special place

Columbine, Paintbrush, and Senecio,
Mosquito Range

I do not think they will grow wild
They take a climate much more mild
It must have taken human hands
To bring this flower to our land

Poppies, along the Yampa River

Where else would be a better place
To park yourself and slow the pace
Perhaps to sit and check the map
Or better yet to take a nap

Parry primrose, along Norris Creek, Mt.
Zirkel Wilderness

A weed we're called we do protest
For certainly we are the best
When color is of prime import
We are unique to any sort

Fireweed, along Schofield Pass, near
Crested Butte

A setting sun doest make the earth
Turn color so to up its worth
For setting suns illuminate
The plants that make our earth so great

Crimson saxifrage, Yampa River Valley

Without the sun the shade besets
A special hue on all that's wet
Without the sun they will not fade
All flowers gain another shade

Indian paintbrush, Sangre de Cristo
Mountains

Who'd believe there was no florist
To cultivate what's here before us
No I paid for neither flower
Twas all the work of nature's power

Wild iris, Wet Mountain Valley

They drink from rain and summer dew
And tend to grow near water, too
Without such moisture there would be
No flowers there for us to see

Mountain bluebell, Sawatch Range

A streak of light pervades the trees
And look at what we barely see
A trio standing tall and proud
To prove that three is not a crowd

Colorado columbine, White River
National Forest

The rocks they try so hard to keep
The plants from going very deep
But here the smallest bit of earth
Is just enough to prove their worth

Mountain bluebell, Mosquito Range

Summer storms they try to make
The rain each day that flowers take
So when we visit their domain
Their brilliant color will not wane

Larkspur beneath the Sneffels Range

A garden here we come across
I must admit I'm at a loss
Just how could nature make this place
The gardener vanished — he left no trace!

Elephantella, Paintbrush, Senecio, and
others, along the Howard Fork of the San
Miguel River, San Juan Mountains

The sun when shining from behind
Lights up the world so we will find
New things we never saw before
And make us feel we once were poor

Fireweed and Senecio, along the
Hagerman Pass Road

Perceptive eyes they see great things
To lesser things do others cling
Perceptive eyes eschew great haste
So look ahead and slow your pace

Forget-Me-Not and Clover at 13,000 feet
above sea level, Mosquito Range

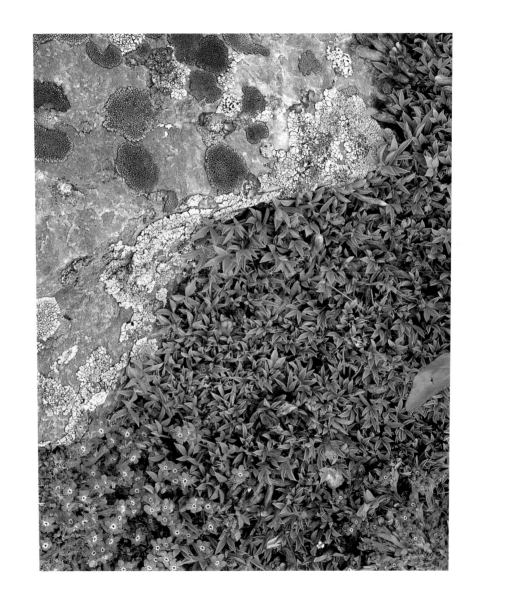

We lay beneath great trees that may
Protect us each throughout the day
For we provide them a great view
We think they know that we are due

Paintbrush and Lousewort, Arapaho
National Forest

Great things do happen here on high
The sun, the rain they both do vie
To be the biggest reason why
These flowers here will never die

Paintbrush, Columbine, Arnica, and
Larkspur, above the town of Telluride